By the Same Author

POETRY
Dyckman—200th Street (Salmon, 1994)
Iron Mountain Road (Salmon, 1997)
The Crosses (Salmon, 2000)
Refuge at DeSoto Bend (Salmon, 2004)

PROSE
From the Sin-é Café to the Black Hills
(University of Wisconsin Press, 2000)

A Tour of Your Country

EAMONN WALL

salmonpoetry

Published in 2008 by
Salmon Poetry,
Cliffs of Moher, County Clare, Ireland
Website: www.salmonpoetry.com
Email: info@salmonpoetry.com

Copyright © Eamonn Wall, 2008

ISBN 978-1-903392-80-5

All rights reserved. No part of this publication may be reproduced or transmitted in any form or by any means, electronic or mechanical, including photography, recording, or any information storage or retrieval system, without permission in writing from the publisher. The book is sold subject to the condition that it shall not, by way of trade or otherwise, be lent, resold or otherwise circulated without the publisher's prior consent in any form of binding or cover other than that in which it is published and without a similar condition, including this condition, being imposed on the subsequent purchaser.

Cover design & typesetting: Siobhán Hutson
Cover artwork: Grunge Landscape by Rolffimages

I sat in silent musing,
The soft wind waved my hair:
It told me Heaven was glorious
And sleeping Earth was fair.

Emily Brontë

Acknowledgments

Acknowledgements are due to the following publications in which some of these poems were previously published:

Crab Orchard Review; *Grasslands Review*; *Poetry Midwest*; *The Recorder*; *Revival*; *Redivider*; *The Scaldy Detail 2007*; *The SHOp*; *South Dakota Review*; *West47*.

"Homework with Her Cat" was originally published in Seamus Cashman ed. *Something Beginning With a P: New Poems from Irish Poets*. Dublin: O'Brien Press, 2004. "Ballagh" was originally published in Jessie Lendennie ed. *Salmon: A Journey in Poetry*. Knockeven, Co. Clare: Salmon Poetry, 2007.

For the poems of South Wexford and the Sloblands, I am indebted to the David Rowe's and Christopher J. Wilson's *High Skies—Low Lands: An Anthology of Wexford Slobs and Harbour*. Enniscorthy: Duffry Press, 1996. For my version of Mirkka Rekola's poem, I wish to acknowledge Herbert Lomas's translation of "(from) Let the Day Be Everything" in his edited and translated volume, *Contemporary Finnish Poetry*. Newcastle upon Tyne: Bloodaxe Books, 1991.

Special thanks are due to Drucilla Wall, Daniel Tobin, Jessie Lendennie, and to University of Missouri-St. Louis for support.

Contents

A Route to Dunbrody	9
Yellowstone Bus Tour	10
Bringing the Pony to the River	11
Stanzas from Mirkka Rekola	12
Slobs	13
All the Worshippers	15
The Heritage Park Reverie	16
Dodge Neon/Li Po	17
Spring Evening with Mocking Bird	18
Ballagh	19
Dawn in Pennsylvania	20
Midsummer's Eve	21
Wordwings	22
Brewery-Millwheel-River Folly	23
Kaamos	25
Of Multitude	26
Lewis & Clark: Omaha, Nebraska	27
Mother and Daughter Aubade	28
The Strangers' Gardens	29
Night Heron	30
Hearing the Ambassador Speak	32
I Was Singing, Tu Fu	33

Homework with Her Cat	34
On Inisheer a Man Walks into a Bar	37
Land & Water	38
The Children Were Eating	39
High Skies-Low Lands	40
Helsinki Sequence	41
In Rainwater	43
Crex, Crex	44
Across Knotted Pine	45
The Bleached Stone	46
On a Tour of Your City	47
The Art of Forgetting	48
The Creels	50
Memorial and River, Boise	51
Hammer Coffee Shop, Boise	52
Basque Museum, Boise	54
Leaving Boise	55

A Route to Dunbrody

Across a calm estuary, we glide over Cromwellian
wreckage to lowland landscape of South Wexford.

Unwearied by purpose, asking no questions today,
hoping, simply, to define King John's battlements

& the broken grandeur of layered, monastic time.
Often at evening, I had driven the Duncannon Line

to catch mackerel off the rocks at Slade, unfolded
sandwiches from foil & twisted cup from thermos

as the ancient lighthouse assumed night's heartbeat.
We traveled, then, rotated by rhythms of making

tides & the necessity of hitting The Terminal Bar
by closing time. Who were my teachers? My gurus

& protectors? I cannot forget single excitements,
swift footraces under arches, the rattle of tackle

boxes, those turnings from the soil to face seaward
the great swell channel, hearts emptied once again.

Today, Dunbrody is our final stop on the road home.
I sit on a stone wall watching waves of barley roll

in the halcyon late afternoon: the weather is fair,
a train passes, my children scamper across ruins.

Cistercians answered each urge to go by staying
put, that insistence I heard often but did not heed.

For guidance from our land, Fathers, I have borne
my children back to your song-lined paths and salted

brooks of Shelbourne. The road ahead will take us
through Shelmaliere West & Bantry to Ballaghkeen.

Yellowstone Bus Tour

Great Fountain Geyser
Fire River and Falls
White Dome Geyser
Tangle Creek
Hot Lake
Celestine Pool/Hot Dog Pool
Mud Pot
Fumarole
Twig Geyser
Coyote in the bushes
Fountain Geyser
Grand Prismatic Spring
Bacterial Mat
Opal Pool
Turquoise Pool
Biscuit Basin
Three Sisters Springs
Moose on the Road
Old Faithful
Dinner at the Lodge
That night
I prayed too
For the trees
That fire
Might spare
A little longer
Their coniferous
Bones

Bringing the Pony to the River

Three Hiace vans and a brown horsebox
—ranged defensively—form an untidy,
Quarter moon. The boys lead a pony
To the slipway, the rising river rippled
By the grooved concrete. Now, a man
Holds absently the reins in an easy hand,
As others, to his side, observe with no
Intent lorries grinding the Wexford Rd.

With old tea-towels and a baby's sponge,
The young wash the pony steady down,
The winter light now fading on an evening
Breathless as a baby's room on a long-
Lost summer's afternoon for all the elms'
Crow beaks and watchman's warm tea,
And disapproval. So still, the pony might
Be made of stone or tickled like a salmon
Into the dead ecstasy of inaction and stopt.

While town folk parade pale puppies along
The smooth white path of the promenade,
Girls and babies hoard quietly near mothers
In the vans' front seats, the pony becoming
the river of yellow light, all shapes morphed
To bright invisibility, men huddled round
A mellow beast, evening iced in winter mist.

Then towels are wrung of the river, hooves
Hupped and clopped to horsebox of human
Histories within all roaming, unwritten still.
Hear the diesel crank of each parked Hiace,
Old published route to hills atop our town.
One sponge set downstream for St. George.

Stanzas from Mirkka Rekola

The nights are no longer warm,
The green tomatoes are cold to their cores,
The sparrows rock empty feeders with fright,
The doves linger forlornly in the low junipers,
The lights of the city thicken the November night.

My grandmother can't shake the thought that some
Thing has been forgotten—a girl's necklace or a wooden
Spoon or the cork sandal the dog rooted from under a table.
The freight train rattles its return to the mines of Wyoming tonight.

The name of the quilt is limewood gate.
Darkness drums incessantly downward beyond dogma
To tenderness softer than millions of moments of snowfall.

My grandmother says the weakest leaves from the maple fall hard,
That a deep blue dream of autumn is a hand under a pillow,
Book on a bedside table, formula from aloe and soy.

The red light from the crossroads darts now on the wall,
Now on the window.

On the wall and on the window.
On the wall. On the window.

When I can put pens and notebooks aside, I will stop time.
Solo, a grey-haired woman stands by an arbor of roses.
Grandmother. Let the day be everything is her reply.

Slobs

Borrer's
salt-marsh
spotted grass,
winter barley
on poldered sand.

Heat wave-summer cars
all beach-bound, alone,
almost, us, on Slobs
among two Dublin birders
equipped with tripods,
lenses, great field glasses.

Five kids, one granny
in pursuit, run riot
upward. We tower
all atop the centre:
wood-formed,
stoneless,
all unconquered,
raring breath of air.

Mud, mire, soft-
fleshed person
written slaba
in Dineen's
backyard.

Then, a birder points to
the vagrant goldeneye,
confirms for me the few
marks I could scratch on
surfaces of these Slobs—
grey heron, little egret,

mute swan, moorhen,
picked from Yeats' verse
and Ballagh's postage
stamps. Then, to close,
my first curlew: children
halted to shout out long
and wild: "I see it."
See it?" "I can see it too."

Soft-fleshed persons
rapt and huddled here:
our common hut on the
hottest day. And all
they had to show—
these patient Dubs gave
away for nought, our
engagement fine as sun
sparkling the mouth's
mild waves. Content
and onward south
now for Tacumshin:
Dub jeep movin' on.

All the Worshippers

All of our ministers are busy. Their churches full
from Bompart to Lockwood. I am walking through

our leafy city, dodging worshippers' parked cars.
To walk is a form of worship as to sit and listen

is a form of walking. Your hymns emerge through
your opened oaks. The Word meets the summer air

when fathers depart with restless children, and I
remain part of the broken world which only at your

peril can you forget. My Methodists, Presbyterians,
Baptists, Catholics, Episcopalians, Jubilee Christians,

so many fill and warm your cool places two thous-
and years on, five hundred since the Reformation.

In another time, I heard old monks chant from high
benches between bogland and evergreens and taped

their song of the sun, retained the *blas* of their wine.
As all of our ministers pray hard for peace, peals of

laughter are carried from opened garages and early
backyard barbecues. To cook is a form of worship,

to laugh a hymn of exuberant annunciation. Stirring
on the air, tart aromas of Sunday coffee that will make

of every house a home, of every heathen one fierce
believer. Sing on heavenly high Sunday, all Missouri.

The Heritage Park Reverie

One wooden ornamental mead hall in dense winter
darkness heralded our beginnings, I had read when

at last, the crooked highway straightened to shape
the tramp's heartbreak. I was walking the road of life

bearing texts, Old English no less, to a rendezvous
with a Limerick girl outside Reginald's Tower, and

fast-forward-back, Hrothgar and Wealhtheow dining
in Heorot where outside loitered a secret industry

of fallow oaks that overlooked hibernation, lurking wild
beasts, monsters of fen and bogland. Mother of the

north. North of Scullabogue, north of Old Ross in
Waesfjord, where I had entered these dark spaces,

and farther on, more north still, to Scandinavia, Finland,
Icelands of denseness, hard vowels, midsummer's

salivations, soldered to lakes and endless pines. Walk on:
crossing New Ross bridge, feet and memory aligned.

Today, the wooden buildings of the Heritage Park cluster
on the estuary's western side. A long ship moored, a gift

shop brimmed with chalices, chocolates, plastic swords.
Once in the hall, someone counted a lover in a rival's arms,

one nipple-soothed infant fell quickly back asleep. I had
crossed the Barrow on my return from a later rendezvous

with a Tipperary girl, walking the road of life on a summer's
day. After Chernobyl, the herd grazed solidly on richer grass:

Two civil servants bore Geiger counters from a marked Hiace.
An unspooled line of thread led straight to Jerusalem's gates.

Dodge Neon / Li Po

Enormously, Explorers and Escalades blossom
on Manchester Avenue.

The used car salesman paces his lot, irregularly,
& the Mississippi is drenched in red.

Sir, one small compact says, you boast that SUVs
are more beautiful than me. But,

Sir, it is at me your customers ogle. Pink Dodge Neon,
purple racing stripes.

Spring Evening with Mocking Bird

A spring night hour is worth a ton of gold.
  Su Shih

The gardener has centered her tomato plants
within pear-shaped towers & now will wait
till morning to remove the last of our marigolds
from front step shade to sunlight-bathed soil.

Her work is as careful as the best translator's:
each flower, vegetable & fruit earning just
the right white space & room to root & grow.
Characters become words, my mocking bird.

Drinking hot tea, we hear our old swing rock
on the whilom, western breeze. Rattle of chain,
brisk bounce to porch frame. Rhythm restored,
like a snoring man recovered—catching breath.

The gardener's hand now reaches for a spoon.
Her green dust spread about our golden gloom.

Ballagh

I.M. Simon Kehoe

This montage finds you sitting on buttercups and grass
On your memory card's faint photo.

Over your shoulder, two banks of sea sand. Between them,
One deep arroyo the spine-thin particles are falling away from.

Overhead, the sun seeks to find its space through low clouds
To bring the sea, over your other shoulder, into quadrille coastal time.

You do not reckon the bounty lost to water; these lone &
Level strands are stretching far away.

You touched the grass when you rested, counted rusted gates
On the journey, quietly pressed your words on the paved streets.

As the sun traced a path, you climbed the old & graded hills.
You heard each measure crafted on this, our slow, brief watch.

Born to a village between Oulart and Enniscorthy, the route
You took to town was your way forward. And the way itself.

Dawn in Pennsylvania

When the revolution ended, a world awoke. Quaker roads traversed flood plains & narrow lanes cut across the fields.

On the rivers, ice melted and horses hugged fence lines of big houses. The provincials were drinking tea in deep forests and open parks.

A neighbor in a soiled shirt sold sweet corn from a roadside trailer. A rustic fence, an unkempt field leading to a red barn.

An old couple posed for a realtor's photograph. A John Deere tractor was parked beside a Chevrolet. A dog was barking.

Travelers sheltered among the horses when emblems blew forcefully across a darkening sky. Men of faith bore leavened bread and ripe tomatoes.

What was scattered was incorporated and horse farms became salty subdivisions. In shaded groups militias shot it out. Silence settled everything.

Midsummer's Eve

The fields are littered with ruins and heartache.

The towns carry the weight of disease and pain.

The great leaders will build a great road across Tara.

The small men in the small towns will fell the last oak.

Wordwings

Enclosed ground of an ancient dwelling house in Ard
Lios, the whitewashed face at oxbow separating the role

of the carriage from the car. High trees, O' Moores,
garth, ring fort, Bloody Mary's plantation: there's a halo

round the moon & wide plains of heartland visible
that say you must listen for whispers still transmitting

from the glossed and runic centres of the word store.
Through brambles and barley at birth you had crawled

to don the world's awaiting tweeds as others on great plains
you had encountered had clung to rock, then trundled stones,

to address the sun from a distorted mouth in the Lakota hills.
Stopping in Arles in mid-July, you again encounter the moment

of your origin on earth: mother, light, language, love. High
above the plains, there's this leaning into blood & bones &

summer's fire though only on the breeze's hearsay can you catch
striped layers as they shift to speak. Look again! Hear the wind's

hot trill. The monk breaks bread with the fairy, the changeling
drinks ale with the lamb, Planter and Gael swap wordwings.

Brewery-Millwheel-River Folly

The folly drove the brewery's wooden wheel
before my years of walking home from school.

To the old people it hardly reckoned as a river
though we believed it nothing less: we had daily
coursed its banks as bands of Iroquois & Sioux.

*

Our fathers had witnessed the great wheel move:
all that we'd observed was water wading under it.

For certain, this moving wheel was another myth
to nobly sit with ancient feats performed on hurling

fields of yore & heroic nights of drinking on the town.
Then, we counted history on each medaled, hoary gown.

*

With a lolly stick I had dug
into tight crevices
around the brewery's outer wall

and bits of quartz and crooked
fieldstone,
I had finger-nailed.

*

Giants of men came to quickly roll the wheel away.
Dump trucks & JCBs came to fill the folly drained.

For how long had the wrecking ball been winding
up to strike that millwheel down?

*

Today, the old people gather on their benches still
to catch the river flowing onward for Wexford town.

Grid-locked streets, Croppy boys & blind referees
pass another hour as interminable as it is sacred time.

I leave them fastened in the month of May to regain
the standing walls I had once touched & to record

old marks I'd scraped into the brewery wall, if these
were feats I'd ever realized at all. One week ago today

in South Dakota, I had lulled a child to bed with the
promise of another Old World tale & then sat an hour
to watch her sleep on the prairie grounds of the Lakota.

Kaamos

The cabin creaked and the roadside ice was low
pink-stem and petal-orange.

A fine crack was etched along the pond's perimeter,
heart now slowed to winter pulse.

The forest roads ran straight through evergreens,
each trail implausible and soft.

And, this lunchtime, the frozen stream outside
the cabin was as indigo as jeans.

She tended a roaring fire and ordered logs. He
rinsed plates and brewed her coffee strong.

Once, the monster Biegolmai scooped the wind
and hurled the snow on Lapland.

Then blinding fury one shovel cracked, the wolf
repaired again to rock and tree.

In that polar night outside Utsjoki the dark-blue glow
of day did seem imaginable and sharp.

Darkness counted: cooker, boot, glove, and all.
At lighted window and high skylight.

Of Multitude

Array of hedgehogs
Catch of fish
Clump of trees
Colony of ants
Down of hares
Flight of bees
Haul of fish
Herd of seals
Hive of bees
Husk of hares
Nest of rabbits
Nest of ants
Pod of seals
Pod of whales
Rookery of seals
School of dolphins
School of whales
Shoal of mackerel
Shoal of fish
Shoal of herring
Skulke of foxes
Swarm of bees
Take of fish
Remember me

Lewis & Clark: Omaha, Nebraska

This morning by the lake geese and ducks
discreetly sit apart and two swans glide
smoothly eastward toward Conagra's steps.
Inside, on drawing boards and in steel
kitchens, chefs created the TV dinner.
The flat-bottomed boat children board
in summer to view a soaring fountain is
tied to its winter moorings. It's below
freezing, a wind blows and leaves scatter
humbly on these lovely walkways. Above,
cast by the bridge, a rocking gray shadow
folds old light into a shiny, new envelope.
When great bridges are sunk in place,
history, our great brown God, is hurled
over gaslights onto the curb, then clothed
in shelter belts—all the way to Kansas City.
Two parallel lines of simple maples form
one young avenue of linkage to 10th Street
and white steps curve soulfully to the lake.
I am walking to a timbered overlook high
above the Missouri River in Nebraska.
Each Spring, scrubs and flood plains swell
again for water raised for its journey home.
Today, each barge captain will intone
Missouri in cadence reserved for the newborn.
Traffic zips back and forth across these free-
ways of pain and possibility we have inherited.
Where boats fought shallows and snags,
miners viewed lands under moonlight and
saw, veiled in mist, islands at dawn. Once,
in a whisper in 1804, Sacajawea was wash-
ing her hair. Lewis was naming this world.

Mother and Daughter Aubade

The architect has curved the great roof and blue neon of the
new arena toward the Missouri River.

At dawn when I awake & pull the blinds, I see a plane
having crossed the river soar over trees high on the Iowa side.

Breezy western light & weird voices cackle nightly
with the talk at my mother's table though, then or now,

like snow geese, the old ground has pulled us back into another time.
There's static: peeled oranges and lemons of daylight

& the sound of the sea at the end of July—on a white evening
bench outside the kitchen door, Old Tom Roberts reads his paper;

pigeons peck at his slippers on an autumn morning; snow falls
on the tall coat stand & front walkway of his block.

Around this kitchen table, folded-in like winter rhododendrons,
my lovely women are gamely sleeping on, light not yet

having flooded with the river our hotel room & I would bet that
the bricks of the streets are as cool & as smooth as their soft faces.

The Strangers' Gardens

When first, outside Albuquerque,
the stranger rubbed rough, cold, piñon pine,
a fierce noon sun cross-cut his skull,

Elsewhere, he had seen gannets dropping
from an open sky and boats reposing
in a forlorn cove.

But, settling among migrants with Sara Gomez,
he would think less each day of tidal waters
and capped sailors.

At twilight, he served an evening meal,
watched her, warmly, wrack wet clothes
before a wood-smoke, open fire.

When they had gone shopping to Alamosa,
he took to examining, many afternoons,
the desert gardens of his neighbours.

One from an arm,
another from a trouser,
two girls pulled.

Hummingbirds gathered at his feeders,
sunflowers sang from his stony ground.
A yellow bus honked from the end of the road.

Night Heron

Night heron
the *Collins Atlas of the World*
eschews was twice recorded
on South Slob's surface:
having,
like Columbus,
flown from center earth
a vagrant route.

Eschews
migration path and famine road
to record
a route peripherique
cut through a field of whey,
and bridges
laid like legs of lego
in lines traversing
ancient streams
and ponds of prayer and plenty.

Eschews
Eala Bhewick
breeding north in Greenland
and arctic grounds of Canada:
come home from Russia
to our Wexford slobs
with love and lore to bear.

Eschews
pale-bellied Cadhan,
brent goose who fed on eel grass
and winter wheat
when tides had buried
in mud
the great and sweet *Zostera*.

Eschews
a long-winged Canóg Dhubh
released
under the yellow
lights of Wexford Bridge
from which for us
our croppied martyrs
swung

to trace blue countries
and spotted capitals:
work of clowns
who turned a trick or two
to move a border here,
a forlorn nation there.

Hearing the Ambassador Speak

Understated weight of evening,
the columns of the university's
recital hall lit to blooming beige,
bunting and drapes are shaking,
slightly so, symmetrical and fair.
Patterned to the seats on which
we fret: Please, Ms. Ambassador,
don't mention our president by
name or frame your thoughts to
wind them down, or up, to the
Iraq War. What a thing of beauty
Helsinki is in this May air, the blue
and yellow buildings that whisper
love and books and Martin Luther,
not him again, as wandering way-
wardly from Unioninkatu to the
the train station, I stop to pass
an hour with students gathered
on Esplanade Park, their heroes
Jimi Hendrix, Janis Joplin and
Kurt Cobain. To the first I pass
from my blue jeans pocket
Lunch Poems by Frank O' Hara,
—"I ducked out of sight behind
the saw-mill"—; to the second
my Missouri driver's license,
permit to meet old bums and
Leningrad cowboys roaring
across American roads; and, to
the third, a "Quick Pick" ticket
for our lottery and $20 bill, just
in case these numbers are not right
aligned with Lady Luck's. She
was charming, that ambassador.
I shook her hand. I walked outside.
Crowds stepped to the *Kauppatori*.

I Was Singing, Tu Fu

Glare from snow
glitter from lake,
fake breeze blowing
full coffee cup.

Last of moonlight
dissolving down:
static water
clogging pools.

A lone goose,
I fly still
between ignorance
and gain.

Know that among
the ecologists,
my name will
never be spoken.

Blood of piggeries
flooded our rivers,
nitrates covered our
fields: I was singing.

Homework with Her Cat

Slowly, she draws books from her lavender bag.
There's Science, Maths, *French: An Introduction*,

& The Merchant of Venice. Each is covered in brown
paper—her mother's touch—& slyly decorated with

leaves, hearts, and daffodils. From the front room,
she hears Dad snore to Anne Doyle on the Nine

O' Clock News. Though it's forbidden, she listens
to the radio through the headphones she has kept

hidden in her pencil case. Outside, through the
kitchen window, she sees rainwater's begun

to form in puddles under the yellow lights in front
of Susan O' Leary's house. She's mean, everyone

says of Susan, and she has a big nose. Country 'n
Western: she turns off the radio, conceals her

headphones so that the wires wiggle in a bevy
of markers. Quickly, out of nowhere, Ghostie

lands on top of her pile of books and copies.
Purring already, and purring more when she pets

him under the chin, & even more so as she runs
the outside of her palm tailwards, along each bony

cheek. If white cats have matching eyes they
are blind, but Ghostie is not blind: he can spot

a robin from a mile away. When it comes to
education, this cat's on top of things. He's

stretched over knowledge as old as Ancient Greece,
as modern as the phrases used by the ultra cool

sophisticates of Gay Paree, nibbling croissants
in cafés along the Boulevard St. Germain. When

she tries to liberate Portia from under his front
paws, Ghostie leaps from the table scattering pens

and papers. After yelling his name too loudly, she
recalls what Mam says: "Nora, be kind to your animals.

They will always be kinder to you than the men
you'll meet." Then, with her ruler, she roots hard

to rescue a red marker from under the cooker.
On all fours on the floor, Ghostie rubs against

her outstretched arm, gives cat kisses to her
nut brown hair. Once, in Confirmation class,

she announced that cats have souls and was
clipped across the ear by Sister Florence. Mam

says all animals, plants, and even insects have
souls and that that's what's called ecology, and

that ecology will save the world from ruination.
Order restored, she makes her Dad a cup of tea,

two slices of toast with marmalade, then wakes
him in time for *Questions & Answers*. With

Ghostie curled in Mam's chair beside the old
range, she flies through her exercises and her

many memorizations, and learns that at one
time they used ducats in Venice though they

spend Euros now like the rest of us. She is
waiting on the doorbell. Mam's yellow fleece

& jet black hair proceeding quickly homeward
from her aerobics class in the Boys' Club Hall.

On Inisheer a Man Walks into a Bar

Gunpowder of our history gathered in his trousers'
ankle-holds, sprayed into the joinings of his pockets—
the clothes make the man, the man makes a nation.

He walks into the opening semicircle of friends, into
dim light, whisper, disavowal, smoke. He knows
that the sea surrounds us and counts for nothing.

I have followed him at the same distance as I did once
my own grandfather when he leaned on his stick breaking
the hard, cathedral climb outside the doctor's surgery.

Outside, oars are bundled in blue synthetic rope &
a single-engined plane circles toward the mainland
where twelve points reach toward known eternity.

The bay's wide mouth, four black boats on the grass,
lobster pots piled like pallets against the wall, listeners
gathered like maize, pushed by the breeze, rattled like

phlegm. Not one word my grandfather spoke did I allow:
none might cross my Maginot Line of salt, pepper and
transparent cruet of vinegar; gone, his long, narrow line

of sunlight with the tide of times I was connected to
in childhood. Last call of hard grandfathers and coarse
history: old men's shoes dusted by sand from that final

boreen. On Inisheer, a half-circle crack displays among
hillwalkers, velcroed cyclists, and rowdy Yanks, one randy
old Republican with tales to roar to the gathered throng.

When Black and Tans fouled the boiling air, the I.R.A
raced, under a moonlit sky, for a Limerick rendezvous.
Granddad bore: a wheel of freedom, and sword of light.

Land & Water

Late now:

the cut body

creaks—

scars

on the surface

of water.

As the forest

shifts

with the wind,

the boat

rocks

on the tide.

As land

lies

with no answer,

water

runs

without time.

The Children Were Eating

Cut sprigs in a Potteries' vase formed a centerpiece
toward which the salt and pepper shakers floated.

*

Cardinals jangled through the low, backyard junipers
that covered with quiet symmetry my old brown fence.

*

Four children held sharp knives to New York strips as
I flew merrily across the room with steamed zucchini.

*

A robin's breast lit the faded red of the bleached path,
a fan flitted rhythmically above our mute, pine boards.

High Skies-Low Lands

In the Norse of these lovely shores,
carn points mark
ragged angles
of our land.
Sound from sand,
timbre from rock,
roots
of polyglot borne ashore
by Flemish weavers
and bearded boatmen
of the great white North:
Irish breasted
to each newborn's mouth.

High skies,
low lands
follow Arthur Young's
and Praeger's paths through
the cropped
republic
of Co. Wexford,
our own young
steps not yet erased,
buried as deep in
slobland sand
as ancient ragworm
rising now
to note, once more,
the long-barreled gun of this retreating tide.

Helsinki Sequence

1.

Kansallismuseo
sled-runner from Lapinlahti:
six men work to ferry children
out across the frozen land.
Under the weakly-lighted
winter sky of a northern day,
they anxiously race for deep
darkness of mid-afternoon.
In each cabin one candle glows
intimately above the Arctic Circle,
all wrapped in one blanket
of silence on top of the world.

2.

As firmly as the visitor's feet
are marked on gravel and stone,
boats mark spaces on water
and flags cuts shapes in air.

3.

Pink and yellow buildings
of the fortress, walking
Suomenlinna, women facing easels,
men locked-on to shutter speed.
The church is a lighthouse, the
light a level below the shining cross.
Light atop light I did
remember when you spoke,
the children's yellow raincoats
from an earlier time.

4.

Across your cobblestones,
under your cathedral
to a café, your voice box
cradled in the flanneled flair,
your slow descending vowels
so much sub rosa whispered fair.

5.

Hear the clank, bell, whistle
of a trolley car, rattle of parlance
from an outside place sounding in.
The Café Engel's brittle spoons
seem shaped from air, the waitress
bowed in secrecy to her customer.

6.

Where now, I ask,
the flare of light,
the light of love?
How will I know
your name?

In Rainwater

They bore metal pails and bottles of Sunsilk outdoors
to bathe in barrels of rainwater filled with summer rain,
the young women. And hung beach towels on kitchen chairs.
They placed necklaces and rings on windowsills of wooden huts
cut into banks of sand, marl, buckthorn: all falling eastward to the sea.

When the bravest dunked her head, her shrieks shot
shivers through the benched throng gathered to observe,
the younger children. August 15. The Feast of the Assumption.
The Royal Showband would hucklebuck the hall at sundown as first
elements of autumn took hold of sweet pea stems, roses, and fuchsia bells.

In turns ungraceful, the young women's heads emerged from water
and massaged with shampoo were dunked ferociously for
the final rinse. The children giggled and were calmed.
Indoors an old man scooped tobacco from a tin
and his smoke worked outward on the air.

One woman ran a toothed brush through another's jet-black hair
while a third, laughing hard, drank from a mug of Lyons tea.
The children turned. The barrel water stilled.
Striped towels strewn on sudsy grass.
White horses bucking on the sea.

Crex, Crex

Stoat
to fence post
posted bill
routed
corncrake
pulverized.

Cans flagons
Bog of Allen
bulldozer
gravel
Dub's
playground.

Diesel plastic
Dunamase
midlands
burning
a mighty
wave.

Citroën
raging
posted speed
hill vale
heartland:
busted ground.

Across Knotted Pine

Her cigarette smoke wound a path through her loosely gathered, gray hair.

She faced us across knotted pine in late-July, under a yellow ceiling among nasturtiums, &

as mirrors cracked in neighbouring towns rain dropped as familiarly into the ocean as before.

No shape held her voice: no hanging ornament, or wooden form. She'd heard

the Word at dawn's turning when the first birds had taken to the air over the vocational school.

As a child addressed in darkness from the silver screen, I feigned ambivalence among the old people.

The yachts rested on the sea. Did we witness broken pieces regaining shape? Green bottles clinking in the yard?

The Bleached Stone

> *They pass by silent, wearing their mourning veils in the mineral whiteness of the streets.*
> Albert Camus. *Exile and the Kingdom*

Now a dulled colour of dried mackerel, my stone lies
bleached on its patio table so that only, in the here of this
crooked morning, a sliver of salt is retained for recoil.

First clockwise, then counter, clothes churn
in a washer, lines on sills being blue, dramas
muraled to the gable retaining their signage, held

between release and restraint as a tide tossing
sand against shore, filling a basin, over the years,
the women passing the boathouse, the sun beating

down on each car of a cortege halted by the door
of the deceased. He is an Arab. The wasps are
feasting and floating in sticky remains of our minerals

while the children are asleep in cool, darkened
rooms away from the noise of the street as the sun,
high overhead, bakes each edge of the yard.

Nauseous and clear as bells ring out across town,
stone from the sea, star of the ocean, man from his boat,
roar of the spin from within and, astringent and right,

there's a prisoner walking to jail still feigning release.
A schoolmaster sits at his desk wringing his hands,
a stone placed by a book on a dry Algerian shelf.

On a Tour of Your City

Hardily, through westward channels & grin gaps &
timbers retaining bottles & cans & under bridges &

below cider drinkers & tied craft, your river, always
within you, enters the western bay. We can't know

its right purpose nor can we count each round cycle
of its time, being distant from its massive lakes & the

rounded stones of its underworld. No more than we
might follow second-hand our own blood's course,

hardened this instant by a school bus shriek to stop.
Under this refracted light, strangers to earth & water,

we walk another tribe's amber-smoothed path to see,
as we depart, sets of tangled wires shaped to save us.

The Art of Forgetting

We recalled then our gatherings on wooden forms:
We sang of no word Grendels, fens, bogs, moors and

ate tough meat in still coarse gardens of anxiety. Then,
a priest regaled for light the sun's dishonesty for Easter.

At the back door of the cottage, where the river spread
into an estuary, a white bench bookended tide and time.

No dust rose from a single road and nothing was heralded
Along the airwaves. Who had jammed the signals, poured

water through the ringing batteries? Each morning then
the watchman found among beach wrack, cracked timbers,

great oars, the body of Halfdane's son gripping his sword,
its handle cracked. Brother of our Finns and Oisíns, their

mounds of earth overlooking the yellow plains and rivers
we had been chosen to forget, that once had flourished

and amiably washed into turloughs deep and open lakes,
throughout the sharp-white wailing north, horsemen riding

quickly to the sea. Our neighbour drives his father's JCB
clearing thistle, grass, and marl for Co. Council housing.

He sits among us to spin this yarn on his father's fiddle
of an invader's bed warmed under a harvest moon in a

crackling lounge, her skin undressed as white as Bríd's.
Who are we, did we recall, the tune's wound figures all

loose and round? Who just can line our wildest space,
old scribes under candlelight in drafty domes called wise

cartographers, or birds and fish cris-crossing cloud and sound?
Joined, if not by name, to Greenland, Norway, Newfoundland,

the fiddler strikes his note to record harder edges of our frozen
fields. Celt, Viking, Norse folk, and all of us remembering all.

The Creels

Two quiet girls rearrange lobster creels

    under the harbour wall,

and, from an outpost of the hotel bar,

    a Country 'n Irish crew

launches into the greatest hits of Margo

    and Brendan Shine.

Four country roads, so the gulls' maneuvers

    seem quite shapeless,

beating fiercely out-of-time, against

    the measure of our ancient crafts.

Hands that shaped the creels,

    the fishing crafts' soft blues,

the fine and slowly sinking light

    at this journey's ravished end.

When all should seem fitted, quieted,

    bedded down for night,

discord shuffles inelegantly onward to the

    rocking cradle and the last crossroad.

Memorial and River, Boise

On Sunday I set out down 8th Street
    to wander
the fine-lined gyres to human rights
    where each shaved
path did undulate then wind, its wisdom
    hemmed in
brittle stone. There Gandhi, Burke—
    old Confucius
and Anne Frank—joined wise Edina,
    aged twelve
of Sarajevo, who in each cut hand had
    held death itself.
Coming from the trees, two cyclists
    whirred over
the iron bridge, and joggers seemed
    steamed like
cattle in winter fields, and the water
    to my touch
was cold as stars. Momentarily,
    this river grasped
the largest stones to halt its run to the
    luring shore
as if to doubt all fonts of kindness
    and good works.
Till like us all, Anne Frank, ratcheted
    down, it ran once more
for its attic, shuttered, ocean home
    where comfort may
not offer safety, nor dissolution rest.

Hammer Coffee Shop, Boise

Late October sunshine walking
along the grove of Boise, great
brown arms cradling the sharp
plateau, for bagels and coffee
from the big man with the big
voice whose small words rattle
the tight tables so that each time
the door opens local papers rise
on the draft, then fall, and again
the espresso machine shrieks up
and up higher than the radio like
Ian Gillan on an old long-player
so I must pretend to read David
Brooks another time, all of these
actions, these rough interruptions,
occurring across the street from
the state capital of Idaho, while
I crane again, one more time,
to hear two lively knitters talk.
I want to know (I'm getting
pretty desperate) why the fair-
haired girl is "pissed with Tony."
To shield from bright light
I lean back, the barista booming
at his shone machine disorders,
his number two piling plates,
cups, on an aluminum metal tray
where they tangle among rolled
napkins and assorted items of
used cutlery like unbound Maine
lobsters in Dierberg's tank, as he
shuffles across the well-worn floor
of this warm coffee shop, along
the grove of Boise, and the clearer

I can discern their faces, the more
scrambled their exchange of news.
Who is Tony—the crafty, cool,
clean-cut mayor of Pocatello, or
a flashy FEDEX driver on the lam
from love these past two days?
He could be a run-down academic
prune visiting from out-of-town?
No Dr. Phil or Carl Jung for sure,
are there some words of ancient
Celtic wisdom I might yet express?
Seated now, between knitters and
myself, with lattes and croissants,
one sharp-dressed lawyer hears
his partner say. "It would be cool
to live in Boise," one thing I did
clearly hear and did not dispute.

Basque Museum, Boise

Affixed to
winter coats,
Basque shepherds,
your tickets
spelled out Boise
and beyond.

Leaving
dawn Chicago,
your train
did not waver
on the plains:
Mr. Jefferson
spun one
crooked wheel.

On a landscape
without shape,
stone boys,
you built
harrimutilaks,
affixed fish
to aspen trees:
fish pointed
to the sky.

To trust
one conductor,
cairn men,
whose language
you did not speak,
in a carriage
among strangers,
was your ticket
to the West.

Leaving Boise

You think the higher you ascend the Sawtooth
    of old Thoreau in Concord
standing still sublime to put America behind him.
    For you, now, these twenty years,
America indivisible from children's names called out
    across a backyard at dinner time,
indivisible from a night in deep December above
    a throbbing street when, finally,
transfigured home, you wept in joy the final hour
    of your wedding day,
finally poised, you knew, for fondness, responsibility,
    and due regard for this America
on whose sheets you stretched, the plough a steady
    sentinel atop the city lights.
When others tugged hemp hoping to pull the liner
    closer to the quay, you waved
so long when it boomed, banked, headed slowly out
    for the shuttered waters of the sea.
And you imagined a breeze that pushed at curtains
    through an open window,
and saw in early June from your kitchen chair a kestrel
    hover above dun autumn brush
on a silver Western afternoon. Today, in the rental car,
    your companions quietly prey
on alpine lakes and evergreens, the houses as we drive
    upward set into pockets of the cliffs,
their conversation bright with longing pushing forward
    above the reservoir of span
then backward into history. We stop in Idaho City,
    in 1865 the largest camp
between St. Louis and San Francisco, where with picks,
    shovels and battered pans,
placer miners scooped pebbles from the streams:
    colours, lumps, and nuggets dinging

into tin: Idaho City, then, a hard ten-hour trip by stage
    from Boise. You attend to
shuttered windows and battered signs, run a hand along
    the shaved façade where
Senator Church declared for president, sounding your
    friends' refrain of sawmills running
without pause, inventing a frontier city to contain—
    on its muddy streets,
and in its provisional, indoor spaces—rushes of miners,
    speculators, preachers, and waves
of no-good hangers-on, bankers, bakers, children
    walked by mothers to shanty schools,
whole families thronged in churches for Sunday prayer.
    Days when the gambler Douglas
dueled Holbrook the congressman, next day dead
    from lethal lead lodged
in his abdomen, shots ringing across town till at last,
    the chambers emptied,
birds resumed in lodge pole pines their mountain airs.
    Inside the old courthouse—
between floorboards—gaps were precisely set to facilitate
    nervous spitters of plug tobacco,
and called before a judge to account for an unpaid debt,
    Mose Kempner wound the IOU
that bore his mark within the sticky wad inside his mouth
    spitting downward into darkness
all frontier proof against his name. Razed by flame in May,
    1867, the Irish
raised a new St. Joseph's Church by Advent's eve,
    climbing wooden steps
to recite litanies and rosaries throughout each civil war.
    Last night, you drank
at the Ha' Penny Bridge in Boise to come-all-ye roars
    of local balladeers
as Irish miners heard ringing in saloons rollicking songs
    of home, thinking as we must,

all of us across time, of many destinies we had managed
    to escape. Not one of us
willing or able to put America behind us so intent were
    we to learn what we did
not know—the tenor of her ways as writ on parchment
    rolls, wired faces, lumps of gold.
You wait by the parked red car at the road's fine curve
    for your companions,
in green shade standing. You think of *Dharma Bums*—
    those kitkats trailing Kerouac
across America, his mother heaving a heavy pack of goods
    across her back,
as his father, running out of hollow breath, chased a train
    continuing, always, to pick up speed.